TRIUMPH HOUSE
Poetry with a Purpose

FAITHFUL FRIENDS

Edited by

Kelly Deacon

First published in Great Britain in 1999 by
TRIUMPH HOUSE
Remus House,
Coltsfoot Drive,
Woodston,
Peterborough, PE2 9JX
Telephone (01733) 898102

All Rights Reserved

Copyright Contributors 1999

HB ISBN 1 86161 583 3
SB ISBN 1 86161 588 4

FOREWORD

A book of poetic tales to be truly treasured - 'Faithful Friends' contains both humorous and heartfelt verse which reflects the love and affection we flourish our pets with and the companionship and dedication they offer us in return, truly becoming our faithful friends.

With tales of fat cats, cat naps, mischievous mice and furry ferrets, this new anthology of verse provides an animated insight into the special pets we share our lives with and the animal antics they indulge in.

A delightful anthology for all the animal lovers amongst us, and it is guaranteed to grace your bookshelf for many years to come.

Kelly Deacon
Editor

CONTENTS

Penny	Paula Doyle	1
Trudy	R J Moulton	2
Little Harry (My Chihuaha)	Dennis Johnson	3
Shep	Cheryl Hier	4
The Donkey Sanctuary	Suzi	5
Friend and Companion	Sheila Thrower	6
Dolphin Enigma	Beryl Johnson	7
My Cats	Eva Todd	8
Performing Puss	Lorna Tippett	9
Camouflaged	Alpason	10
Almost Everybody Has A Special Friend . . .	Karen Dalglish	11
Blue Budgie	Cheryl Setchell	12
The Terrible Twosome	Nikky Braithwaite	13
The Contented Cat	Frank Jensen	14
My True Love	Lynsay Brockhill	15
Silence Is Golden	Rita Hardiman	16
I Am Just A Cuddly Cat	Kathleen Y Ambler	17
Twinkle	Steve Kettlewell	18
Butch Cassidy And The Sundance Pig	Euphemia McKillop	19
The Hunt	Lynn Catherine Noblett	20
Suzy	Julie Brown	21
In Memory Of A Little Dog	Jack Judd	22
The Chimpanzee	Nishani Balendra	23
Rula	Joan M Crow	24
My Pet	Pamela Pratt	25
Tess	Susan Lee	26
Tallulah	Ruth Daviat	27
Midnight Stallion	Sarah Levene	28
My Dog Thumper	Gemma Eastwood	29
Stray	Sylvia M Harbert	30
Laika	Kopan Mahadeva	31
Smokey	Sally Shaw	32

Morn Cogitations And Deeds Of A Moggy	Hilary Jill Robson	33
My Four Fiery-Furred Felines	Annette Heap	34
More Or Less	J R Catlin	35
A Family Cat	Marylène Walker	36
Birdland	Jack Conway	37
A Happy Girl	Margaret Jackson	38
Times We've Seen	M Hartley	40
Chester	Richard Ninnis	41
Carpet Chameleon	Kenneth Neil Stirling	42
My Cat, Smurf	Emily Salmon	43
The Black Sheep Of Lynsore Upper Hardres Kent	P Harrison	44
Our Cat	S K Clark	45
Tina	Ann Forshaw	46
Twin Souls	Mena H A Faulkner	47
Chip	Alexander Robertson	48
Smartie	Mary Ward Hunt	49
Lisa	Terry White	50
Snatch The Springer	Jean H Fox	52
Roddy - The Unsung Hero	Len Fox	53
Last Day	T M Brown	54
Nocturnal Pastime	Stephanie Berry	56
Memories of Mysty, A Feral Cat	Helga I Dharmpaul	57
In Days Gone By . . .	Jeannie Price	58
Somebody's Pet	May Walker	59
A Real Mate	Chris Key	60
Green Woodpecker	Grahame Godsmark	61
Pony Talk	Heather Henning	62
Sam	Irene Benyon	63
Feline Remedy	Coralie Campbell	64
Tinker, Our Cat	Janet Lancaster	65
Cobwebs Undone	Ann Copland	66
A Faithful Friend My Cat	Doris Davis	67
Leo	Elaine Waite	68
Tommy	Peggy Howe	69
Pipsi	Raeesa Khan	70

Paws For Thought	Sandra Edwards	71
'Saffron Sunset'	Denis Martindale	72
A Doggy Tale	Bessie Thackeray	73
My Errant Blackbird	Joan Weston	74
Ivory	Christine Nolan	75
The Nightlife Of A Tom Cat	Thomas Splitt	76
A Vision	Rex A Dawson	77
Nicky	Emma Lampard	78
Lady	Jack Major	79
The Birds	SNIKPOHD	80
The Sentry	David Leese	81
Our Dear Ben	Brian MacDonald	82
A Man's Best Friend	Sam Stafford	83
Tamsin	Helen M Seeley	84
My Companion Dog	Poppy Ashfield	85
The Dogs Of Cromer	Alan J Titley	86
My Cat	C Allsop	87
A Tribute To A Tabby (Dikum)	Sam Royce	88
I Wish I Was A Fish	Roger A Carpenter	89
A Dog's Life	I J Wickert	90
Ode To An Old Cat	June Thompson	92
You Think You're So Superior	B P S Weldon	93
Toby	Anne R Cooper	94
In Sally's Eyes	Tracy Brierley	95
My Border Collie	Christine Clark	96
Pig	Mike Parker	97
I Follow A Dog's Behind	E C Inkpen	98
Pussy Cat	J Mary Kirkland	99
My Friend Simon	Babs West	100
Epitaph For Roli	Patricia Weitz	101
The Dachsie Pack	Betty Robertson	102
Tsara	Paula Fox	103
New Thing	Susan Ann Higgs	104
To Beth	Mary Ford	105
Our Dog Bess	Daisy Ellen Jones	106
My Cat	Dora Watkins	107
Flossy	Beryl Sylvia Rusmanis	108

For Mishka And Sasha (My Beautiful Cats)	Anita Richards	109
My Dog Duke	M W Lowe	110
My Special Friend	Emma Gale	111
Gazehounds	Francis Arthur Rawlinson	112
Deva	June Burden-White	113
My Little Cats	M Muirhead	114
Lucky	S A Buckingham	115
Fidelis	Rosie Hues	116
Daddy And The Fish	Terry Cutting	117
Beauty	Evelyn M Rose	118
Snowball Came	Dolly Harmer	119
The Adorable Six	Linda Roberts	120
This Dog	Jean Turner	122
Bob	Hild	123
It's A Dog's Life	Robert Jennings McCormick	124
'Titbits' (By 'Bounty' Guide Dog Puppy . . .)	Lynda Burton	125
Jessie Faithful Friend	Christine Peers	126
Eulogy For A Feline Person	Anne Sanderson	127
Hit And Run	Andria Cooke	128
Almost A Lion	Audrey Woodall	129
Good Dog, Nice Dog!	Gordon P Charkin	130
Suzi	Gloria Pocock	131

PENNY

Oh how nice it is to have a friend
Who'll never drive you round the bend
A friend who laughs with her tail
Who seems to know when you're feeling pale
A friend who stands on all fours
Who has mastered the trick of opening doors
Who barks when she's happy and whines when she's sad.
When leaving her alone she makes you feel bad
Who knows when to run and when to come back
Who will playfully open any tied sack
She's black and she's clever and without a doubt
She's someone I could never live without.

Paula Doyle

TRUDY

Our poor old dog has passed away
for fifteen years a friend.
Like all God's living creatures
her time came in the end.

She didn't have a pedigree
or prizes by the score.
Her parents were quite a mixture
but we loved her all the more.

We miss her head upon our knee
her bark and wagging tail.
The titbits when we had our tea
the morning post she brought without fail.

For days she rode on the tractor seat
in the heat of the blazing sun.
Mowing, turning and baling
it really was her fun.

She loved to walk down by the woods
and chase a rabbit from sight.
She never really caught one
but she gave it such a fright.

They say a dog's a friend for life
and I think that this is so.
Because an empty chair and basket
make you miss them when they go.

R J Moulton

LITTLE HARRY (MY CHIHUAHUA)
(Dedicated To My Wife)

He was a happy little chap who loved to sit upon my lap,
His eyes were black and shiny bright, his coat was soft and brown and white.
His heart was big and swelled with pride when he was walking by my side
Strutting out upon his lead so everybody would take heed.

His love was clear for all to see, so gently did he stroke my knee.
Exuding all his loving charms, just asking to be in my arms.
Oh how he loved his brother Flash, the pair of them cut quite a dash.
For Flash 'n' Harry were a case, and brought a smile to many a face.

He loved old Mickey, Rowley too, and chased them round the garden new,
His joyful nature knew no bounds, when he was playing with those hounds.
Alas too soon, I was so sad when illness struck my little lad,
He was so brave and fought his best, but in the end he went to rest.

And so Great Master in the sky, cradled his arms for him to lie
Cosy and warm and free from pain, to join his friends there once again
So now the time has come to part from my Chihuahua, bless his heart.
I miss him so, but dry my tears, remembering the joyful years.

Now in the Elysian fields he plays in golden sunshine, all his days.
And when, at last, he needs to rest, he sleeps upon an angel's breast.
But sometimes in the still of night I feel a softness, brown and white,
A gentle paw upon my knee, my Harry's not forgotten me.

Dennis Johnson

SHEP

You with your boundless energy
my furry hurricane.
You ask so little back from me
for all my many gains.
I often muse my little friend,
had our paths never crossed,
Just where would your life story end,
how much we'd both have lost.
I well remember that first night,
I brought you home to stay.
You whined for others out of sight,
that farmyard far away.
I listened as your restless din
echoed within my head.
Sense told me stand fast don't give in,
I pulled you to my bed.
These days you take it as your due
when on my bed you lie.
Though chided for allowing you.
Do I care? No! Not I.
Together we are as a team
you are my company.
I share with you my thoughts and dreams,
respect your loyalty.
Yours is the bright enquiring face
that greets when work is done.
You are the clown who loves to grace
my lonely world with fun.
Laughter that only we two hear,
the clown, the dreamer know.
And love will keep us ever near,
though time deems you must go.

Cheryl Hier

THE DONKEY SANCTUARY

We went to see the donkeys
My family and me
We've been there several times before
'Cos we get in for free.

There were donkeys in the cow-shed
And more were in the yard.
Lots were grazing in the fields
And a few were working hard.

Some had names upon their brows
And collars round their necks.
Some had notices that read
'I'm a nervous wreck!'

A tiny donkey pulled a cart
Filled with girls and boys.
Round and round the indoor school
Then for a picture poise!

A little shop was full of stuff
Like posters, pens and books.
And everywhere all you could hear
'Don't touch son - just look!'

Hunger said 'It's time to eat.'
So we sat down by a field.
But donkeys like boiled eggs for lunch
The things weren't even peeled!

The day went far too quickly,
We had to say goodbye.
The donkeys watched us leave 'en masse'
then breathe a great big sigh!

Suzi

FRIEND AND COMPANION

Although my name is really Leonora
Leo my mistress calls me -
my coat is black and shiny
much softer it could not be.

I am a very lucky dog
for my master and mistress live in the Downs.
We take some lovely walks together
sometimes almost to Eastbourne town.

I never chase the sheep
but a rabbit now and again -
I never catch them they are so swift.
It's fun though all the same.

My mistress says I have lovely eyes
a beautiful soft brown -
there's silver and grey on my nose and chin
a handsome Labrador all round!

Occasionally when I am naughty
those eyes are then downcast -
they chastise me and I am truly sorry
but soon all is forgiven fast.

Sometimes I have a special treat
a visit to the sea -
and here I splash and swim and play about
there never was a happier dog than me.

My bedtime is 10 pm
cosy blankets have been mended -
master comes and tucks me in
another happy day has ended.

Sheila Thrower

DOLPHIN ENIGMA

Dolphin
confined to the blue pool
for man's pleasure
swims ceaselessly round and round,
racing, diving, jumping
providing therapy and thrills.

Would so many tears shed
over its plight
wipe away the smile
on the face of the dolphin?

Beryl Johnson

MY CATS

I have two lovely little cats
one is ginger, one is black.
One named Cleo, one named Max
and boy do they my patience tax.
Both are loving, both are kind
Both are hunters to my mind
some days birds, some days mice.
Though I try to tell them that's not nice
still they both are very young.
Lots of years to have more fun.
At least I hope that this is true
I'd be really lost without my two - cats.

Eva Todd

PERFORMING PUSS

Rolling around on the grassy lawn
is one of Billy's delights.
An area of grass he sprayed for his own
no interloper to poach.

A red red robin came hopping along
his intent to play.
Peering at Bill unperceived
perched and tweeted, having his say.

Damp was the grass, really quite wet
provoking Bill, his mood to get set.
Stretching a paw, in playful pursuit,
the robin he swiped at, attempting to dent.

Flying, perching, swooping
his display made Billy ponder anew.
Raising his paw to dap once more,
as the robin played his cue.

Missed once again, poor Billy
after all, robin started first
Billy only wanted the whole thing in reverse.

A squirrel through the fence
was viewing the scene.
His eye never leaving the spot
Bill and robin, playing (tweek you)
Boy, oh boy, what a plot.

This little game, continued some time
Mum called Bill inside.
Holding his head, with infinite pride
Billy bowed to the robin
and walked inside . . .

Lorna Tippett

CAMOUFLAGED

Strong winds blow golden threads on a rippled grey sand
particles surging - united in song
but, there's a solidness
camouflaged perfectly in the hazy sun.
The sand and the coat almost become one
moving incessantly in a bodily form.
Bounding and jumping then sleek as a fox
playing in excitement with the stormy sea
reflecting the emotion, laughing with me!
Sometimes you're not just what you seem
you camouflage lightly your canine ways.
An ivory shell snapped between lily-white fangs,
a prize which she gently releases to my hand.
A soot black nose at the ebony 'weed
patiently waiting before we proceed.
Floppy brown ears like two waved-smoothed stones,
glistening beard like the fleeting spindrift.
Twin winkle shells gleam amber from granite
set at the front for the wolfhound to prey.

Alpason

ALMOST EVERYBODY HAS A SPECIAL FRIEND...

If I had a pet . . .
you could be someone to talk to.
To share my problems with
to celebrate my happy moments
and to cherish in my joy.
You will be curled up on my lap
watching our favourite soppy film.
With boxes of tissues and chocolates.
You will be there when I am sad
and use your ears to wipe away my sadness.
I promise I won't be mad
if you knock over my coffee cup.
Or find your hair on my favourite jumper
or when your hair clogs up my
vacuum cleaner and it short circuits.
You will scare away the prowlers
and chase the neighbour's cat.
We'll take walks in the park
my obedient and faithful friend.
I'll watch you splash in the bath
and shake water all over the bathroom.
And when the rain pours down
we'll sit by the fire and I'll stroke
your soft creamy coat.
But if you were my pet
one day you would leave me
and I would be filled with a
great sadness . . .

And then I couldn't use your ears
to wipe away my tears.

Karen Daglish

BLUE BUDGIE

I brought you for her
in my younger days.
To ease her loneliness perhaps.
I hope you did.
I'm sure you did.

We loved you too, Ben
Despite your noise.
Your mixed-up songs,
mimic with no words.
Wolf-whistles and chirps.

When she left us
I took you home with me.
To comfort my new loneliness
And so you did
And how you did.

When you go too, Ben
I'll miss your noise.
Your mixed-up songs
And I'll think of her
And miss you too.

I've stored the pain
For that day.

Cheryl Setchell

THE TERRIBLE TWOSOME

Creeping onto the bed
and cunningly stealing the duvet,
they leave me shivering and cramped.
One paws my right arm
whilst the other generously
gives my left ear a wash.
One black and white, a true collie,
herds imaginary sheep when he
takes me for a walk.
The other, black and tan;
of curious mixed parentage
and brimming with puppy exuberance.
He chews everything not nailed down.
They curl beside me on the sofa;
muddy paw-prints everywhere.
My hands are full, stroking both
and brown eyes gaze sleepily.
They dream until dinner-time.
Joyful barking echoes around the kitchen
and I think they smile at me afterwards.
I smile back at my terrible twosome,
my love for them reflected in adoring eyes.
I wouldn't have it any other way.

Nikky Braithwaite

THE CONTENTED CAT

May I introduce myself, I'm Mrs Campbell's cat
My ancestors were wild but I'm the opposite of that.
We're supposed to be nocturnal, so the feline experts say.
They must be wrong for I can sleep as well by night or day.

My coat is thick and furry for when the weather's dire,
But when the chill winds blow outside I stretch out by the fire.
My claws are curved and long and sharp, for catching birds and mice.
But that's hard work, and anyhow, that sort of thing's not nice.

I don't need to hunt for food or rummage in a bin
My food is always brought to me from my favourite tin.
Sometimes I get a special treat, a tasty piece of fish.
Nicely cooked and served up in my willow-pattern dish.

I have these special eyes designed for prowling in the dark.
I did prowl once and then I only did it for a lark.
In the evenings when my owner has her quiet little nap
I rouse myself enough to jump and curl up on her lap.

There's just one little issue over which we disagree
Whether I belong to her or she belongs to me.
But either way, this is the life (actually I've got nine).
If any life is full of bliss I have to say - it's mine!

Frank Jensen

MY TRUE LOVE

You express your love to an animal
the same way you express your love to a man.
You can talk to an animal
the same way you talk to a human being.

Your love towards an animal
can not be said enough times.
Your love towards a man
is priceless towards the love you give your pet.

Your pet has earned its love
through your trust.
Your pet is your lifetime love
so you can chuck your man and keep your pet.

Lynsay Brockhill (14)

SILENCE IS GOLDEN

Crotchet are you mute? Have you no meow?
When you want something you can still show us how,
Look up into our faces and rub around a leg,
Go to where your food is - you don't have to beg.
You might have a problem but you can adapt quite well,
So we know where you're hiding, will you wear a bell?

Crotchet we love you, whether you've voice or not,
We enjoy your company as you give us such a lot.
I know you like to taunt us by jumping on the shed
And acting difficult to get - so cross words may be said!
You play with toys so happily, take an interest in all things,
For you it's all experience, from cabbages to kings.

Crotchet you've a lovely purr that readily comes on,
Just a few melodious bars and our hearts are won.
Your trust in us is simple that we won't do you harm.
But we'll provide a haven of love, joy and calm.
Having a little handicap doesn't make you less.
For by overcoming it, you show you are the best.

Rita Hardiman

I Am Just A Cuddly Cat

Us cats can be wee cuddly things
Or scratch you with our claws.
But we're not trying to show you
That you cannot be boss.

It's just that we have our special needs
Of scratchy pads and food;
And then you'll be so very sure
We cats can be so good.

Give us just a cosy place
Where we can lie and sleep,
And we will give you in return
A love that's rare and deep.

I'll give you friendship you won't find
Amongst your human friends.
For I am just a cuddly cat
'With a listening ear to lend'.

Kathleen Y Ambler

TWINKLE

Twinkle, twinkle, my little star
what a true friend you really are.

When companions are vacant
you're always there.
In the chilly winter nights
you show that you care.

A tiger some call you
yet you have no roar.
Such a tame little puss
you're the treasure I adore.

Without you I know
I could not live.
Your tender affections, and the love
that you give.

So Twinkle, Twinkle
my treasured little star.
Thank you most sincerely
for being the friend that you are.

Steve Kettlewell

BUTCH CASSIDY AND THE SUNDANCE PIG!
(The Tamworth Two)

Three little piggies went to market
Two little piggies ran away
One little piggy got the short, sharp shock,
The other two decided not to stay.

They legged it from the abattoir
Their little loins were shaking.
They knew that had they stepped inside,
They'd chop them up for bacon.

So they darted through the village,
Their assassins close behind.
They swam the swollen river,
Just refused to be assigned.

But those piggies won the Tamworth chase,
After nine days on the run.
Then the villagers decided
That keeping piggies could be fun.

We might as well just keep them now,
And treat them as our pets.
So now those little Tamworth Pigs
Are reprieved with no regrets!

Euphemia McKillop

THE HUNT

can't you hear
the hounds' barking
horns' blowing.
Oh, run fox run!

can't you hear
the horses' hoofs
trampling the ground.
Oh, run fox run.

they're close behind
you haven't a chance,
find the strength to
Run fox run . . .

Lynn Catherine Noblett

Suzy

Suzy came into my life
a little waif and stray,
From the moment I saw her
I knew she was here to stay.

With dark shining eyes
and ears turned down at the tops,
White tip to her tail
and four little white socks.

With a nature so charming
she's found herself a home,
A life full of love
and a place to call her own.

Julie Brown

IN MEMORY OF A LITTLE DOG

The silent call made in your mind
to someone who no longer hears.
You look to see if they are near
but only shadows can you find.

You sense you feel a presence there
a faint scratching at the door.
Echoes of sounds once heard before -
pattering paws upon the stair.

His feeding bowl but lately bought
reminding now of those few days.
You had to know his winsome ways
a fleeting gladness - come to naught.

Jack Judd

THE CHIMPANZEE

She was found in a cage
no bigger than a box room
this six foot chimpanzee,
she was used for testing
and had smoke pumped into her lungs,
she clung to me
this chimpanzee,
she wouldn't - couldn't - refused to let go
and resign herself to her fate,
poor thing,
I held her and protected her
and would never let go
of her, my chimpanzee.

Nishani Balendra

RULA

My dog's name is Rula - and by jove she does.
She's a bundle of fun that gives off a buzz.
Rula chases the coalman and window cleaner too!
And anyone in a uniform she gets in a stew.

She has a little ball which is her delight,
And takes out my hubby to play every night!
No matter what the weather Rula's out there,
Hail, rain or snow our Rula doesn't care.

She's soft and fluffy and so full of love,
And fits on my knee like a hand in a glove.
She has her own chair and is cosy and warm,
Quite content until it's time to perform!

Rula knows all the days and where she'll be at,
Any sign of a doggy bag and guess who'll be sat?
Watching and waiting with wild little eyes,
'Where's my food?' she almost cries.

Tummy all full then in front of the fire,
This little dog you have to admire.
She'll roast for an hour then come up for air,
And head for the door without a care!

She is my best friend without a doubt,
And when I call her I've no need to shout.
She loves me and guards me without a moan,
My pride and joy, this dog that I own.

Joan M Crow

My Pet

I have a friend loyal and true
One so loving, there are a few.
But mine is special, I am sure
Wait until I tell you more.
We share life's ups and downs
We share pleasures and any frowns.
We go for walks or ride in the car
Seaside is first but often not so far.
Playing games with squeaky toys or a ball
Help with the digging, no trouble at all
A long black coat, glossy with care.
Baths in the shower, water everywhere
Towelling is old hat, shaking is best.
Chased around the garden, labelled *a pest!*
Good food and a basket with rug so snug
Makes a dog contented, when sealed with a hug.
My pet is looked after and it's not hard
For a faithful friend who is always on guard.
Protecting from strangers who are kept at bay
By a black barking monster having its say.
Soft brown adoring eyes are a sure sign
Wagging tail, deep sigh, shows all is fine.
Then on the sofa while watching TV
Cuddles and kisses for my master and me.
This is my way of thanking my friend
Who can be counted on up to the end.

Pamela Pratt

TESS

The most precious thing now in my life
Since I lost my darling wife,
Is my faithful sheepdog Tess
Without her my life would be such a mess.

The long walks together that we take
Thru' the fields and down to the lake.
I close my eyes and see her still,
I never knew that she was so ill.

She never said how bad she felt,
Whilst at her bedside that I knelt.
Thru' the long hours when she was dying
Trying not to let her see me crying.

But just when I feel it's too much to bear,
Tess jumps up onto my chair.
Licks my face as if to say
Don't worry we'll see her again some day.

A more loving companion I couldn't find,
The most sweetest nature, so caring and kind,
She means all the world to me
And I to her - as all can see.

Susan Lee

TALLULAH

You, Talullah are the child that died;
indeed a cat you will remain
but you obviated tears I cried
for chances not to come again
yet neither child nor adult be,
merged between mystic and a sphinx;
are they mirages, love, you see,
your thoughts like those some Guru thinks?
You infuse my shifting dream with light,
from slits moves honey-yellow sheen,
after toil you'll solace me tonight,
my warm yet enigmatic queen.
Sometimes, Talullah I am reborn
with you my dark, enduring sage
and myself some vulnerable spawn
needful of your mature age.
My bosom fills not with mother's milk
with which to feed envisioned mite
but Talullah puss, your coal black silk
recompenses barren plight.
Enormously you philosophise
and just as ardently bestow
an affection that to my surprise
I feel in deepest debt to know.
Talullah, velvet slippered sleuth
so often scrutinising me,
fathoming out the naked truth,
how well you gauge my frailty.

Ruth Daviat

MIDNIGHT STALLION

Charging through the darkness
like a cloak of fire he came
with hooves of jet black ebony
and seafoam tossing mane.
He covers ground in no time,
he gallops on effortless till
he reaches the end of the world
then swings round to gallop on nightly still.
The sparks setting fly burn a lyric
on grass that his smoking feet tore.
The eternal pounding, a night lullaby,
the strain that his champion heart bore.
With fantasy wings on his broad back
he rears then canters the sky.
He flexes his streaming banner-like tail
and glances the world passing by.
He lives for the night and the moonbeams,
he dances without needing rest.
He prances and spins in the shadows
then charges - a starlight express.
He will gallop on always eternally
and rule forever as king
and his journey will always be Pride of the Night -
whatever the morning may bring.

Sarah Levene (13)

MY DOG THUMPER

He barked and barked
At the crack of dawn,
He made me laugh
He made me yawn,
He played and played
Throughout the day.
He gave me hugs
Although he tugged.
I'll love him for eternity
And although he's not here,
I know he still loves me.

Gemma Eastwood

STRAY

Little stray cat, you look so ill.
I have prayed for you, that's as good as a pill.
That God will restore your fur
In the meantime, a tin of tuna, I will incur.

To give you some oil and make your coat grow.
It's two weeks now, an improvement, you show.
Your eyes were weeping, I bathed them with milk
You're not so mangy, your fur's not yet like silk.

Your mouth was festered, I can't look inside.
You need to go to the vets for a ride.
I can't take you, so we must rely on God.
He will make you well, and do a good job.

Because he loves animals, as well as people
He helps the sick, the weak and the feeble.
Independent pussy cat, you're very aloof
But I have won you over, love is the proof.

Sylvia M Harbert

LAIKA

With doubts it might be a toy daubed with pitch -
A victim of children's curiosity -
I picked up and rescued it from a ditch
Of Colombo's Municipality.

But *it* became a treasured parcel of my life,
Participating in my every bit of strife.

What else was there, of that four-legged she
That warranted a piece of poetry?
The answer can't in a few words be said.
It has to be felt and perceived, instead:

Her eyes that talked, paws that stroked, her unfailing
Love that was fond, understanding, forgiving,
With instinctive concern for my well-being . . .
Her wags, her wails, her uncanny common sense
Which seemed to surpass human intelligence . . .

She was cold and unyielding to canine suitors -
Seemed her wish was to live for my better or worse
As my good maid, geisha, mother, darling daughter,
Pet, consoler, playmate, life-giving air, water.

She, and Goddess Muse were my only mates.
When I spent two whole years within Woodville's gates
Till one day, 'Miss Frisky' jumped our eight-foot wall
To chase a Jaguar on the road to Galle
In the Pearly Island. And, when Laika died,
Not only I, but my wife and kids too cried.

They said, the innermost cells of their hearts bled
When they learnt, in England, that Laika was dead.

Kopan Mahadeva

SMOKEY

A little girl of twelve years old and I was pony mad
I never gave a moments peace to my poor mum and dad.
And so full of excitement when on that October day
We went along to buy for me a very special grey.

A two year old New Forest and not yet broken in.
Both of us so much to learn and now we could begin.
We'd found a field to rent and we'd purchased all the tack
And when I earned his trust Smokey let me ride upon his back.

We'd hack for miles in those early days, he gave me so much joy
Proud head held high, ears pricked, he was such a handsome boy.
Smokey had a favourite place where he would like to be
He loved to ride across the marsh and gaze towards the sea.

Tractors, pigs and fences were the things he really used to hate
And when he wanted to escape Smokey used to jump the gate.
Dad and I would search for him whenever he would roam
Till we moved him to the Common and he finally felt at home.

Childhood days have gone now and how the years have flown
And suddenly I am married with children of my own.
Twenty seven years passed by and Smokey's bones grew old
He looked a little thinner and began to feel the cold.

I was so very far away the day my old friend Smokey died
I couldn't make it home in time to be there by his side.
But not for him the indignity of being towed away
We buried him there on the field next to where he lay.

There's another pony grazing now on the field where Smokey
used to be
He has no need for grass these days - his spirit is running free.

Sally Shaw

MORN COGITATIONS AND DEEDS OF A MOGGY!

Jump on their bed! Leap off!
Vault on again! Take off!
Wake up! I'm up! Get up!
Quickly please because it's late.
You'll be sorry, I can't wait!
Will you obey? You will! Okay! I'll lead the way!

Follow me! Oh! Just a mo!
I've a stowaway in tow!
Stay awhile, let me scratch, it's a flea I must despatch!

It's away! We'll wend our way!
Hey! My toy mouse, let us play!
I'll spring! You let it swing!
Wily cat and mouse sparring.
A left and right! What a fight!
Now must go! I'm dancing to avoid overflow!

Bound downstairs, along the hall.
Come! You're walking at a crawl.
Ears flat against my head, concentrating to be fed!

Waffle! Nuzzle! Reached my cupboard!
I soon learn, I'm no sluggard!
Sniff! Checks fine! That tin is mine!
What a feast for a feline!
Is it ready? Famished! Scurry!
Jump up mewing, pawing. Worry! Hurry!

Open catflap! Back in a trice!
Know my 'brekkie's' something nice.
Just a throw of life's dice that I live in paradise.

Hilary Jill Robson

MY FOUR FIERY-FURRED FELINES

Ginger was a pompous puss
Lucky was not so.
Puss-puss never made a fuss
Nor put on a feline show
Tigger was a charming cat
A pure delight to see.
Never raised a talon at that
... Well certainly not at me!

Annette Heap

MORE OR LESS

We bought a pretty puppy
A terrier white and black
The *More* we tried to call him
The less he would come back.

Our mum just liked to nurse him
Visitors, he did not amuse
And dad just smacked and cursed him
'Cos he piddled on their shoes.

Gran just poked him with her sticks
Which made our *More* - more mad.
She said with those two knobbly bits
He always would be bad.

Dad took him to the vets today
He didn't say what for
Now mum and dad are happy
And I call him *Less* not *More*.

J R Catlin

A Family Cat

Believe me, I can muse
On her favourite pastime
Of cajoling her kittens
With tales of thunder
And lightning, and hiding
In cubby holes hardly
Big enough to let
One mouse turn round
      And run . . .

Marylène Walker

BIRDLAND

It's strange when one doesn't expect too much
How often one's agreeably surprised.
With no more thought than seeing birds as such
In plain surroundings, hardly advertised.
I entered Birdland just to pass an hour
To find I could have cheerfully stayed all day.
What joy and inspiration - penguin power!
Majestic, rhythmic poise in bold display.
What peace, sheer relaxation came to me
As I saw kings and pawns in harmony.
The swan in smooth perfection, even paced
All happy souls who know that food is placed
Twice daily by attendants full of care.
Another feature which for me was rare
Were humming birds with their unusual sound;
So small, no less attractive though I found.
An hour I spent - it now seems so much shorter!
Idyllic time at Bourton-on-the-Water.

Jack Conway

A Happy Girl

Lucy's such happy girl
love radiates where're she be.
Sparkling eyes which captivate
a faithful friend to me.

Snow and sunshine she adores
a tinkerbell, mischief to make.
Carries slippers round the house
so craftily to take.

Chasing round the garden there
how those butterflies really charm.
Missing nothing in her sight
face so cute restores calm.

Shake a paw, lie down and sit
tail a-wagging great fun to share.
Fetch the ball to throw again
spreading cheer everywhere.

Snuggling ever close to me
this a favourite resting place.
Comfort, warmth always to give
such loving, gentle ways.

Twitching ears and nose to see
when in dreamland so fast asleep.
Then a whimper also hear
she'll squint and take a peep.

Velvet ears, a chocolate coat
face so cheeky, expressions speak.
Affection always freely shown
those treats ever to seek.

Such fine greetings everyday
an intelligent Labrador.
A special babe very dear
in my heart evermore.

Margaret Jackson

TIMES WE'VE SEEN

Farewell to you my Revel, my horse, my silent mare.
Today I keep a memory, of days we used to share.
I told you my deepest secrets, and all my problems too,
When grave or gay, you stood by me, you were a friend so true.
We made a lovely picture, as you walked through life with me,
On some sad days you would carry me, and set my burdens free,
And now as you sleep peacefully, for they had to end your pain,
A picture comes into my mind, and I'm with you once again,
I weep for you my Revel, and as I sit and dream,
My tears are for those happy days, and those special times we've seen.

M Hartley

CHESTER

'Why don't we have a dog?' you said.
'All right.' I said. Easily led!
'I've seen just the one,' you said with a smile.
'Not far from here! Just over a mile!'

So off we went, kid's quivering with joy.
'I want a girl dog! No! I want a boy!'
We arrived at the kennels in a very short while.
'Here we are,' you said, with a smile.

'I have six puppies for sale!' the lady said.
'They're out the back, in the little shed!'
With baited breath, we opened the door
And saw six baby Yorkies, on the floor!

Five were all scampering, so full of fun.
And up in the corner, was this little one!
All alone, and shivering with fear,
Cowering away as we came near!

Tenderly I picked up the poor shaking mite.
I passed it to you, it was love at first sight!
He looked up at you, snuggled against your chest.
We never bothered to look at the rest!

We took him home, he settled in well,
He was really happy, I could tell!
Chester we named him, I'll never forget.
For twelve years, he was a wonderful pet!

Dear Chester has gone now, we miss him so!
But he's still with us wherever we go.
He gave us his love, unreserved, sincere.
We feel a lot richer, since Chester was here!

Richard Ninnis

CARPET CHAMELEON

Back in nineteen seventy three
I bought a lizard cute and twee.
It changed its colour readily,
To blend in with the scenery.

And being nineteen seventy three
Carpets and curtains were garishly
Made in patterns quite unearthly,
Quite tasteless decor it was, you see!

Now my wee lizard, cute and twee
Ran straight across, quite easily,
Our garish carpet wild and free,
Then disappeared quite speedily.

I couldn't see him on the floor,
I panicked so I closed the door.
I stared so hard then stared some more,
Where had he gone! My eyes were sore!

Some fifteen minutes; there was he!
Appearing by my right hand knee
Unblending from the scenery,
Of mother's garish carpetry.

So there he was! He wasn't gone.
I realised just what he'd done.
I looked so fondly on that one
Wee lizard like he was my son.

Kenneth Neil Stirling

MY CAT, SMURF

A month ago she was happy
Now she's gone away.
She was lying there dying,
She's gone, I wanted her to stay.

Now we've got a new cat,
A moggy black and white.
She eats as quick as Smurf did
And jumps with all her might.

She chases the rabbits round the garden
She never hurts them though.
She protects them, when stray cats come,
Keeps them safe from harm.

So did Smurf, she was lovely
Couldn't hurt a soul.
The new cat is just like her
Never vicious, never slow.

The thing about the new cat
Is when I look into her eyes.
I can't help but think,
I've seen them somewhere before.

Emily Salmon

THE BLACK SHEEP OF LYNSORE UPPER HARDRES KENT

Galloping flock racing to greet
eleven black Welsh mountain sheep.

Across green fields magpies' and larks'
yellow amber eyes stare afar.

Long swaying tails sketching their paths
sniffing, nibbling sharp blades of grass.

Quivering backs, absorbing sun
trespassing red fox on the run.

Molars crunching hips, mouths to hay
all through the year and every day.

P Harrison

OUR CAT

Our cat curled comfortably upon the chair
Feeling the warmth of the fire there.
We come and go, she doesn't flinch a hair
Not one of us would move her, we wouldn't dare.
There she sits all comfortably without a care
With one eye opened, gives a disdainful stare.

And when she decides it's time to eat
She stretches and then jumps to her feet
And you, you'll have to jump up from your seat
And feed her the very best of meat
And don't forget to give that little treat
And then she'll return to snuggle on her favourite seat.

S K Clark

TINA

You were so very cute and small
In your early puppy days;
Oh so full of mischief
And funny playful ways.

I taught you many clever tricks
You were so very bright;
I could never catch you out
You always got them right.

We'd go out walking together
Or in the car to ride;
It seems no matter where I went
You were always by my side.

When you had your operation
I held your paw all night;
We had a very special bond
Which throughout your life burned bright.

You'd comfort me if I was down
In your own magical way;
You'd lick my face, give me your paw
And by my side you'd stay.

You were a mongrel, a dog of all kinds
With fur, eyes, nose all brown;
But to me you were the cutest dog
That lived in this here town.

So here I pay my tribute
Telling of the times that we did spend;
And all the treasured memories
Of you, my canine friend.

Ann Forshaw

TWIN SOULS

He sits upon my willing lap
This lovely, grey-blue Persian cat.
My shadow, guardian, constant friend
Who follows me in faithful trend
In all my ways.

His eyes half-closed in ecstasy
He looks, and there for all to see
His love in amber bowls embrace me
And our twin souls are met and held
In enchantment.

From ages past we've seemed like one
Long, long before the world begun.
His features neat, leonine bland,
The lion there to trace, as grand
He sits with regal air.

His purring soft, so deep and sure,
A breed from generations pure
A Lomond Blue his mother Queen
Of cherished cats with royal mein
To greatness born.

The living toys of Queen and King
To give them pleasure and to sing
With true affection, endless song
To those who loved them for so long
In olden times.

Now he lives content, that other self,
Who knows me as I know myself
And when his span of life is done
We who have always lived as one
I know will always haunt my path.
My dear, majestic other half.

Mena H A Faulkner

CHIP

You have been a trusted companion
You listened when I was down
There were times I thought
You actually understood me just from a frown
We would share biscuits and tea
When you sat next to me
Forever by my side
We'd go for runs
And larks in the park
Playing fetch 'n' peek a boo seek
What more could a boy
Who's unsure at the world
Ask from a companion or friend
Never thought the time would end
Now you're an old man that's true
Not so energetic on your feet
All tasselled and grey
And maybe a tad deaf
But you're still there
With a wag 'n' a sniff
You have been a trusted companion
You listened when I was down
There were times I thought
You actually understood me just from a frown.

Alex Robertson

SMARTIE

Quiet of a night he comes
and brings me his mouse,
a toy to amuse him
as it runs around the house.
He finds my old slippers,
a great hiding place
for a little grey rodent
with dust on its face.
I pretend not to see it
as I pick up my shoe,
and the mouse gives a squeak
and leaps wildly in view!
But how can I scold him?
My blue and white boy
who brings home his treasures
for us both to enjoy!
Dear Smartie. He came to me
a tiny wee scrap,
too small to reach up
and climb on my lap.
I fling wide the door
and away runs the mouse,
now peace reigns once more
in my little thatched house.

Mary Ward Hunt

LISA

Once she was free
A cub with a future to be
That's how I see her

No jungle or plains
But a jail with no chains
For sad Lisa

She paces her cell
Like a soul lost in hell
She's so lonely

Her eyes cast afar
As the wind kisses the bars
So coldly

Standing regal and proud
She cries out aloud
For her freedom

No tears depart
But deep in her heart
She keeps them

They come and they stare
But what do they care
I feel for her badly

An African sight
Eyes yellow and bright
Now gaze so sadly

Tears fall to my shirt
I see the pain and the hurt
I long to free her

But like a star bright at night
Keep your spirit held tight
My sad Lisa

Terry White

SNATCH THE SPRINGER

Snatch, Snatch cuts a dash
without a doubt he has no match.
He came to us - his head held high,
His hunger knew no bounds.
He was so thin it was a sin
and yet he was so proud.
Now at last his hunger gone
his love comes shining through
in us he has put his trust so
we must see what we can do.

To show him how we love him now
to watch him run and play.
Joy in this our canine boy
he gives us day to day.
One year on we still have a way to go,
Patience and time on our side,
with a character to guide.
Snatch, Snatch - really cuts a dash
there is no doubt, he has no match!

Jean H Fox

Roddy - The Unsung Hero

A tiny ball of fluff
was how he came to me
but soon that tiny pup
was bigger than a tree,
and Tabby just next door
to him was deeply rude
for each and every day
she'd nibble at his food.

Gently he would nudge her
and send her on her way
but still into his patch
she would ever stray.
She really was a nuisance
but he would keep his cool
for feline girls he knew
could be stubborn as a mule.

One day she had a litter
where foxes ever stray,
She was too weak to help them
as they blindly made their way.
The vixens came to take them
but Roddy was on hand
and against the unfair odds
he bravely made a stand.

He saved those little kittens
but suffered for the cause
and as he sighed his last
they lay between his paws
and that's why every day
- a hero he will stay.

Len Fox

LAST DAY

Come on girl
whistle call
expectant wag of tail
eyes bright, ears erect
jingling lead on collared neck
good girl.

Sight of open woods
delight
rejuvenate stiff old limbs
pounce and leaps of joy
through fallen leaf and pine
impaired vision follows sound
unknown to mine
good girl.

Rabbits, birds - all flee
as streak of canine flesh pursues
nose pointing, panting breath
excites and whets the appetite
good girl.

Returns at call
slow gasps and wheeze
tail listless back from trail
no trophy this day
good girl

Energy spent no restraint
last effort bright
soft brown eyes dimmed, then no more
to fairer woods I pray
good girl.

Tears flow unchecked
for last farewell
to aged faithful friend
good girl
Mrs T M Brown

NOCTURNAL PASTIME

Stealthily slinking
on moonlit prowl.
Dark oaks locating
brief hoot of an owl.
Soft paws padding
on dew dampened ground.
Tail flicking, ears twitching
alert to each sound.
Pouncing on rodent
with deft paw and skill.
Torturing playtime
enjoying the kill!
Onward through darkness
a fight and a growl.
Claws scratching, teeth biting
an enemy's howl!
Stars fading, moon dipping
a bound up a tree.
Hoping, observing,
the first bird to see.
Sun rising, now yawning,
through garden to creep.
Door opening quick greeting
to basket - to sleep!

Stephanie Berry

MEMORIES OF MYSTY, A FERAL CAT

A purr, a hiss
A mother's kiss.
A lick, a paw -
That's what I saw.
As I peered into the nursery.

A black fur ball,
There're four in all.
Joyous delight!
A mother's pride
Did I behold in the nursery.

So full of joy -
A girl? A boy?
Milk for their meals.
Then a rest Mum steals.
Cuddled up inside the nursery.

Where is this place
So full of grace?
You may well ask.
Find it - my task:
My garden shed is - the nursery.

Helga I Dharmpaul

IN DAYS GONE BY ...

He ran to the door when a visitor knocked,
Now he raised his head, ears slightly cocked.
He leapt for joy, or a stick or a ball
Now he sits and watches when you call.

His eyesight is poor, his pace is surely slow,
But there's an undisputed fact that all owners know -
He's a true and trusted friend,
The kind you'll want to treasure
So watch him now enjoy
These golden days of leisure.

Jeannie Price

SOMEBODY'S PET
(For All Our Little Friends Up There)

He lies there so still by the golden stair
Just a little brown dog with shaggy hair
But he lifts up his head when footsteps draw near
Still hoping that well-loved voice he will hear
Then soft comes the whistle that he knows so well
Now the waiting is over it's there to tell
A scamper of feet and a bark full of glee
'I knew that one day you would come to me.
You will find secret ways I'll search for them too
What fun it will be to go walking with you!'

May Walker

A REAL MATE

My name is Whisky, I'm a rough-haired Jack
and when I was little, I was brought back
to live with this family, who loved me a lot.
Even when I was naughty, I deserved all I got,
but it made me learn and I grew up real good.
I began to behave like a smart dog should.
I had to get used to avoiding wheelchairs, though
as my little mates, Sharon and Haydn began to grow
worse on their legs, but I didn't mind
I knew they needed me to be loving and kind.
I fetched them the letters when they fell through the door
and I picked up the papers from the floor.
I got little treats and more freedom to roam
with a comfy chair and settee, made myself at home;
My mates grew up and one day something went wrong.
All were upset and Haydn was in bed, so long.
I lay by his side and he talked to me
and deep down I knew, this wasn't meant to be.
The he was gone, his room empty and sad
My young mate, seventeen, his illness got so bad
But I had to love Sharon, she needed love and care
And by seeking attention, I let them all know, I was there
They hugged me and talked, tears often fell too
But as time passed by, things got better, less blue,
Now I'm getting old and I sleep quite a lot
But I'm real proud of this family I've got
Because I'm one of them, life really is great
I know I'm a dog, but I'm their real best mate.

Chris Key

GREEN WOODPECKER

Thickset and squat
In his dark green jacket and scarlet biretta,
Beating a muffled tattoo on the yielding turf,
He probes my lawn.
Flicking his tongue he picks off the scurrying ants
As a fairground marksman topples the sitting ducks.
He eats his fill.
Sated at last, with a farewell yaffle of thanks
He takes his leave, lifting over the laurel hedge.

How can he know the joy his presence brings
More than repays my hospitality?

Grahame Godsmark

Pony Talk

'Please tell me, my friend, for I need to know:
How do I make a pony go
On a Saturday morning?

I've broken a twig and asked him to walk.
Will he come with me? No, he will sulk
On a Saturday morning.

I've slapped both his sides and told him to trot,
He puts back his ears and says he will not
On a Saturday morning.

I'm wasting my breath with all kinds of banter,
I can't persuade him even to canter
On a Saturday morning.

Why won't he gallop? The words that I use
Make him toss his proud head and simply refuse
On a Saturday morning.'

'Oh no,' said my friend, 'you won't make him go
By biffing and beating and blaming, you know,
On a Saturday morning.

You must soothe him and smooth him and call him your pet,
Kindness will make him the best pony yet
On a Saturday morning.'

Heather Henning

Sam

Dear Sam, my four-legged friend
For seventeen years you gave me love so steadfast and true.
Now I am so lonely without you;
No other could replace your faithfulness and trust
You followed me from one room to another,
You felt you must.
Because you knew my disability, and cared for me so much.
Now you are at rest, the flowers on your grave are in full bloom.
They seem to be saying, I am still with you in every room.
God bless you dear Sam, I know God has a place for you.
And I know He will take care of you, as you did for me.
Morning, night and noon.

Irene Beynon

FELINE REMEDY

Should he leave you
and deceive you,
Get a cat.
She'll bring you
comfort, joy and much elation.
In fact she'll be
the purr-fect consolation.
Although at first
I doubted this,
Like you,
I got one,
And I've proved
It true!
In fact she's number one
In my affection,
The purr-fect antidote
For any rejection!

Coralie Campbell

TINKER, OUR CAT

Tinker arrived in a handful of fur:
A tiny sweet kitten with appealing purr.
Quizzical and naughty, he taught us to play!
We buttered his paws to persuade him to stay.

He grew up in stature and conquered our hearts
He safaried *his* garden till he knew all its parts.
He terrorised birds and once captured a mole!
He climbed up the willow like a flag up a pole.

He visits the neighbours who all know his face.
He has fights with his rivals, and hisses in chase!
If we can't find him, he'll hear Peter's call:
He gallops, and in like an aimed cannon ball!

He has regular habits, and last thing each night.
He demands *roly-polies* then we say *goodnight!*
In the mornings he greets us: his loudest *meow-wow,*
He seems almost human with this melodic *hell-ow!*

Now he takes life at a steadier pace:
He snoozes contented in many a place.
He toasts on the boiler, he glows in the sun:
But he seeks a warm lap when our day's work is done.

Tinker isn't immortal - but as long as he lives
We should thank God each day for the joy that he gives.

Janet Lancaster

COBWEBS UNDONE

Spin me a yarn, whirl me a reel - filmy pattern
Arthropod interlacing binding your spiry silken web.
Revolving winding threads to capture your penance prey
In a reliable fabric sinewy and strong
Spellbinding - skilful spider working vigorously
A tradition nature only gave you.

Cobwebs hanging like drapes - pelmet nets
From a dilapidated murky off-white ceiling - membranes
Tough and resistant productive occupies weaver
Only to be encountered unawares
With the tough wiry bristles
Of a broom - obliterated.

Trapeze artist dramatising on a fine wire line
Until one escapes in a rush
Returning to more rivalry and hostility
Stamped on intensely probably
Beneath wheels or a giant obstacle
On the end of a powerful limb
Squashed unwittingly to a mushy pulp
Like many other creatures - inconspicuous
Small with delicate features.

Ann Copland

A Faithful Friend My Cat

A cat can be your greatest friend
from all life's troubles be a shield.
You can with it every secret blend
knowing it will never be revealed.
It knows when you are feeling sad
or when you are filled with joy.
Will share all times both good and bad
and knows every whim it can employ.
Knows how to make you do its bidding
soon shows it rules the roost
takes over your life - no kidding!
But gives your confidence a boost.
Will confiscate your favourite chair
or curl up on your bed.
All your furniture cover with hair
and is impatient to be fed.
Will demand your full attention
never accepting second best.
Will make sure it gets a mention
when being compared to all the rest.
A cat will stay with you for life
a good, loving home is all it asks.
It will gladly share all your joy and strife
as long as in luxury it basks.

Doris Davis

LEO

Bedraggled and crying, there is no denying,
you were the cutest kitten we found.
You needed a home, when you were all alone
and settled in our family home.
We care for your needs, and in return,
you learned to love us and trust us.
On cold winter days, in bed we lay
under the duvet no fuss.
You snuggle up tight, without a fight,
content in your own little world.
You purr in my ear and twitch in your dreams,
Your the most loveable cat that I've ever seen.
Where would I be, without you on my knee?
Your voice announces every arrival.
We will always be here, so you've nothing to fear,
Waiting for you to return.
Soon you'll be three and goodness me
a strapping ginger tom you've grown.
And the days you appear with frogs, birds and mice,
I'm usually the last person to moan.
There is one thing I'll ask, and this is the last,
please leave the fish to swim.
I know you like water, this we have found,
stay out of the pond, it's out of bounds!

Elaine Waite

TOMMY

I never knew from whence he came,
but on my doorstep he'd remain.
He was not young, he was not old,
how could I leave him in the cold?

Matted fur, and ears all torn,
looking hungry and forlorn.
What could I do? But ask him in,
To leave him out would be a sin.

I found a blanket, made a bed,
somewhere soft to lay his head.
Gave him food, milk to drink,
in the morning - I must think.

Should he stay? What should I do?
The answer I already knew.
This pussy cat had love to spare
and knew that I would really care.

We took a visit to the vet,
all checked out, now we were set.
Tins of fish, toys for play,
this was just a purr-fect day.

He stayed with me both day and night,
rarely wandered out of sight.
He ruled my life and stole my heart,
then came the day we had to part.

He gave me such a lot of pleasure,
his memory I'll forever treasure.
I'll thank the Lord for ever more,
for sending Tommy to my door.

Peggy Howe

PIPSI

Nails sharp,
Ears high
Paws tiny,
Whiskers long.

My baby little hamster,
Is the noisiest in the world.
He crawls up your shirt on and on
He bites holes in your clothes.

Fur soft,
Teeth white,
Tail short,
Fur patched.

He's worse than a ferret,
He climbs up your trouser legs,
The most cheekiest hamster there is and . . .
His name's Pipsi!

Raeesa Khan

PAWS FOR THOUGHT!

A kindly nuzzle with my cold moist nose,
Means do not fret! Everything will be all right.
A rolling snarl warns strangers beware,
though I'm toothless I'll still try to bite!

I'm a Yorkshire Terrier named Pebbles,
my ancestors once eradicated rats.
Now I boldly patrol the corners of the garden,
where I thrive on chasing cats!

I rise every morning at half past four,
and prepare myself for the long day ahead.
But as soon as my owner goes out to work,
I sneak back into bed!

I have frequented the doghouse
more times than I would like to confess.
Personally, I thought the paw-print design was rather fetching,
which I stamped on my owner's white dress!

I guard my companion religiously throughout the night and day,
she seems to understand the things that I try so hard to say.
And when she is feeling poorly,
Overwrought and emotionally low,
I snuggle up and love her in the only way I know!

Sandra Edwards

'SAFFRON SUNSET'

We decided on this special name
When we saw our poodle's coat -
His ears were tinged with apricot flame,
As was his chest and his throat.
What a shy young puppy Saffron was -
I taught him to climb the stairs.
And I was relieved by this because
It helped overcome any scares!
So, with practice, he'd climb up and down!
Into each bedroom he'd run . . .
He'd lick away at each morning frown,
Waking us up one by one!
Most of the time he was well-behaved,
Good-natured and grateful too!
But oh how he hated being bathed,
Sighing till drying was through!
Saffron was groomed with clippers and comb,
Transformed, fluffed up, safe and sound . . .
He'd shake himself off when he got home
Just like the happiest hound!
He'd love learning tricks - to sit and beg,
Such a loving dog was he . . .
To shake our hands he'd stretch out a leg
In faithful gentility!
But time moves on . . . and sweet Saffron died . . .
And we miss him to this day . . .
He was our joy and he was our pride . . .
Till the sunset that took him away . . .

Denis Martindale

A Doggy Tale

Key in the lock
Open the door
To be greeted by a friendly paw . . .
Excited whimper - a wagging tail
Feet all going, chewed up mail.
Mischief in his eyes, waiting to play
He's soon forgot you've been away.
Now for a mad dash
A look for the lead
A slipper there, he tries to retrieve.
Tail still wagging
A bone at your feet
Then its ears to attention for walkies,
A land of adventure, what is to be found
His nose on the ground.
Walkies all over, back home to sleep
Laying on his bed, a golden heap
This is Sammy
Dreaming doggy dreams - their best friend.
Willing to please . . . Phew!

Bessie Thackeray

MY ERRANT BLACKBIRD

If you saw him in my garden
Standing quietly on the lawn,
You'd think he was the most
Ordinary blackbird ever born.

He does the normal blackbird things,
Collecting worms from dawn till late,
To feed his brood in the bush nearby
And take care of his mate.

He serenades me from the tree
In his lovely trilling voice,
The notes cascading through the air
That make my heart rejoice.

But my neighbours say when he visits
He is not nearly so polite,
He sits on the fence and stares at them
Swearing with all his might.

I really don't know what makes him
Behave like a rude, spoiled brat
And then add injury to insult
By continually dive-bombing their cat!

Joan Weston

IVORY

Our cat just loves the heating,
By the boiler in her box she stays,
All winter if we'd let her,
In a warm and cosy haze.

She treats us with contempt,
In a cold but loving way,
She never exerts herself at all,
And we know that's how she'll stay!

Christine Nolan

THE NIGHTLIFE OF A TOM CAT

What a curious time of day is night!
No one seems to like it, all get fright.
But out here in the dark somebody moves,
The owl who searches quietly for his prey,
Seeking out mouse and shrew for his meal.
But someone else is moving in the dark,
A killer just as cruel and capable.
Old Tom Cat too, he seeks the mouse and shrew
And often has to do it for a living.
What banshee wail, what scream erupts at night?
It's our old Tom Cat out there with his mate,
Producing kittens by the score and if
They're lucky each one finds a comfy home.
What mystery in pussy that he prowls
The night? What drives him on? What urge?
You'd think the deils of hell were all quite near
When pussy screams and screeches in the night.
But sitting at the fireside where it's warm,
You'd never think he had that funny side.
He looks content as every pussy should,
And if he's going to purr, give him some food.

Thomas Splitt

A Vision

We went in secret, in the depth of night
When there was none to watch us, not an eye
Save the lone dweller of the lonely sky
To gaze upon the little sylvan glade
Wherein we knew his resting place we'd made.

When the white moon had robed us in its beam,
We thought some vision of a blessed dream
Or spirit of the night before us stood
And held communion with us in the wood.

Her countenance was beautiful and kind:
About her golden hair the moonlight played.
She spoke - her voice was softer than the wind -
'Your little Bruce is happy now,' she said.

Rex A Dawson

NICKY

'We're going to Nan and Grandad's, Emma,'
'OK Mum I'm coming,'
Put on my shoes and pull on my coat,
And down the stairs I'd go running.

In the car I'd be so excited,
The thought of you running up to me,
The feel of your wet nose on my face,
You were such a delight to see.

Feeding you chocolate drops,
I'd share them between us,
You didn't like dog food from a can,
Spam and eggs were your favourites.

You loved to run up and down the green,
We'd play with you all the time,
You were Nan and Grandad's dog,
But in a way you felt like mine.

Now, whenever I see a black Labrador,
My memories return, of you,
Of happy days when we were both young,
And all the things we used to do.

Emma Lampard

LADY

You shameless hussy, unfaithful jade.
You wag your tail and lick my face
Swearing love and undying devotion.
Along comes my wife and you do the same.
What is your game?
And yesterday I even saw you lick the postman
                                            lucky chap.
I am going to change your name.

You shameless hussy, unfaithful jade.
You roll over on your back
And show your front for me to scratch.
Then I find you do the same
To every Tom, Dick and Harry,
And even Aunty May
I am going to change your name.

You shameless hussy, unfaithful jade.
I throw the ball for you to fetch
Looking forward to a game.
You catch the ball and gaily carry
It to some stranger up the lane.
I am going to change your name.

You shameless hussy, unfaithful jade.
In my study I quietly sit
With you beside me on the mat.
I look up and feel a twit
To see beside my wife you're sat.
I am going to change your name.

Lady I love you all the same.

Jack Major

THE BIRDS

They come into our gardens,
The robins and the tits,
Attracted by the bits of bread,
The bacon rind and nuts.

That we leave on the table,
That is for them designed,
They look at us as if we're daft,
We are just the human kind.

The pigeons come they stand aloof,
They perch above the car.
They leave a deposit on it.
They go a bit too far.

The magpie comes, sometimes the jay,
The others disappear.
They come at different times of day,
Each season of the year.

The blackbird and the thrush,
Are noted for their song.
The starlings in their pin striped suits,
Then come and strut along.

What would we do without the birds,
Who bring to us their booty.
We would need a thousand words,
To describe them in their beauty.

SNIKPOHD

THE SENTRY

Some homes have red alarms fixed boldly to their walls,
Or signs to warn all salesmen of their unwelcome calls,
But our alarm is Harris, the defender of the flock,
A brave and fearless fighter, our blue-black bantam cock.

From morning rise to evening roost, he's on a guard patrol,
To protect his female followers, his one and only goal.
His heart is strong and steady - he has no crow for 'No',
For though he's only bantam weight, he'll tackle any foe.

His armoury of war is conventional but sound,
And launched at any challengers who chance to be around.
The alarm crow is succeeded by a thrusting running charge,
Sharply followed with a fearless peck, and flying spurs at large.

He proudly struts around the lawn and flower beds all day,
Surrounded by his hens, except when they go home to lay.
He clucks the flock about him, when food comes into sight,
For slugs, and worms, and hedgebugs are culinary delight.

The brilliant sheen of plumage, provides a colourful display,
With reddened comb and wattles, his standard in the fray.
Other neighbours adorn their lawns with fearful plastic gnomes,
Ours for fearsome Harris, is both fortress and home.

David Leese

OUR DEAR BEN

Our dear friend Ben has passed away and left us sad and tearful.
We miss his furry presence still, his nuzzles by the earful.
We miss his boisterous energy, his busy body stout,
His bouncy walk, inquiring look which asked, 'When are we going out?'

The post, milk and window men now arrive without a worry
That their presence will bring forth a burst of pretend, quivering fury.
Our cushions sit just where they should, no longer squashed by Ben
Perched on their top to see what's what and who and why and when.

When on our walks, the trees, the grass and all the other plants
His nose no longer quizzes with sniffs and snorts and grunts.
With tail erect and ears alert, his jaunty stride showed you
Just who was Top Dog - and who was leading who.

His bark no longer greets us when we arrive back home
Though his mate Piggy does his best to show he's here - but all alone.
Our bed stays made, the cats unfrayed. It's all so very still.
Ben's not around to guard the ground and keep us safe from ill.

We hope there is a heaven in which we meet once more
The furry friends we've loved long since and who have gone before.
May they give us a welcome when we are 'gathered in'.
For waiting there is
Smoky, Henry, Rusty, Max
And, lately,
Our dear Ben.

Brian MacDonald

A Man's Best Friend

Upon a hook, on the kitchen wall,
Hangs Rover's lead -
A scallywag, known to all
Who lived within our pleasant street;
A little marvel on four feet.

We knew he never learned to read,
At lampposts where he always peed,
Ignoring signs, that did indeed,
State, 'dogs must be kept upon a lead'.

His lineage, we never knew,
His coat was black, his eyes were blue,
And never still, without fail,
Wagged his long and bushy tail.

Now he has gone to his canine rest,
Of all our friends, he was the best -
For him, the midnight sun has set,
But Rover's name - We'll not forget.

Sam Stafford

TAMSIN

Tamsin stands at the end of the drive -
Black and white elegance of grace and beauty.
Watching and waiting for Claire to arrive,
A self-appointed sentry on duty.

White-spatted feet and black coat sleek,
Tall and slim with neat Van Dyke beard.
Quietly aloof in his 'uniform' chic,
Unpurring, unstirring till Claire's step is heard.

Golden eyes watch her approach with pleasure,
Back arches lithely in an act of greeting.
He shows his affection in self-restrained measure:
This one act reveals a cat's joy at the meeting.

He follows Claire in with contented sigh -
The vigil now ended that proves his devotion
Pencil-slim tail held proud and high,
Silently moving with liquid motion.

Helen M Seeley

My Companion Dog

Swinging hips and wagging tail
Brown liquid eyes and debris trail
Mouth so wet and teeth that grip
Tidy room is now a tip
Head used like a battering ram
Affectionate greeting from dog to man

Sandy coat short and thick
Soft velvet ears - with one great lick
This animal we can't ignore
As he stands at the door

He's waiting, and it's no surprise
For his daily exercise.

Poppy Ashfield

THE DOGS OF CROMER

North Norfolk is renowned as the haven of the hound,
   A paradise for pups, who reign supreme.
Round them, routines revolve, as their 'doggie' lives evolve
   (To onlookers, at least, so it would seem!)

Here they come, the more the merrier: First two spaniels, then a terrier,
   Then a Labrador, behind a young Alsatian.
A ginger Chow, a-bristle, heeds his master's warning whistle,
   And icily ignores an old Dalmatian.

Even when they're good, they're oft misunderstood;
   A man's best friend can end up in hot water!
Perhaps it sounds inept, but we humans must accept
   That doggies *will* do things they didn't oughter.

In a gale, the furry hat (of sable, mink . . . or cat!)
   Which adorns the well-groomed head of Mrs Perrett
Is blown into a tussle with a semi-blind Jack Russell,
   Who *thinks* he's sunk his teeth into a ferret!

A Doberman named 'Scheldt' makes his hostile presence felt,
   When the postman, bearing packages and letters,
Beats a panicky retreat down a quiet, tree-lined street,
   Pursued by 'Scheldt' plus two enraged Red Setters.

Dogs are a breed apart; they learn their route by heart -
   - They always seem to know just where they're heading.
Mother, following on, tells her offspring: 'Sally! John!
   Slow down - and do be careful what you tread in!'

We ought to give due credit to the character who said it -
   - The Immortal Bard (not Chaucer, Keats or Homer) -
Who, in his halcyon days, penned this poignant little phrase:
   'Cry havoc, and let slip the Dogs of Cromer!'

Alan J Titley

MY CAT

Your fur is thick with bugs
And there's cat's hair on the rug
You tell me you want your feed
When I am trying to read.
You're chasing with your ball
Up and down the hall
You put me to the test
Making all the mess.
But if you have to see the vet
You're my very special pet
You're the body on the mat
You're my lucky cat.

C Allsop

A Tribute To A Tabby (Dikum)

A sound has gone from daily life
It leaves a numbness now,
An illness made a friend to die,
I'll cope, but know not how

The purring from a feline friend
Poured out in life to me
Has stopped, and left just happy thoughts
Of what she used to be

I treasured her with tabby fur
And wettened nose, well cold
Her cuddly ways and playful days
Remained till she was old

At fourteen years in feline terms
It spelt out Ninety-eight
She had to go one day for sure
And pass her 'golden-gate'

I miss her purring sound around
And times she made for play
The click of toys against the walls
Pounced on and knocked away

But now alas, she is no more
A well loved Cat at rest
She gave her all and had a Ball
One of the very best.

Sam Royce

I Wish I Was A Fish

Little fish, swimming in a bowl
Round and round, without a goal.
Part of the world, and yet apart,
Finish the circle and then re-start.

I watch him and he watches me.
I envy him, such harmony.
His food, like manna from above.
Content, he has no need of love.

Someone told me long ago
Fish can't remember, just don't know,
What took place a second past
No memory, so nothing lasts.

But that's the curse a man must bear,
The love I've lost's not dimming.
Oh how I wish I was a fish,
His life consists of swimming.

If I close my eyes, I see your face,
I block my ears, but can't erase
The sound of laughter from your lips.
I guess this fish has had his chips!

This room becomes my own glass tank.
I gaze through windows, and I thank
My lucky stars I'm safe inside,
No obstacles, I'll not collide.

I'll simply swim around and then . . .
Perhaps I'll swim around again.

Roger A Carpenter

A Dog's Life

The March wind, it is blowing,
Blowing every day,
I certainly don't like it,
And I won't stay out to play.

I look out through the kitchen door,
A dustbin lid goes by -
And several other items
That I can't identify!

I really do not like it,
I just shiver and shake,
Mum says that if I carry on,
An Aspirin I must take.

That's not all the story -
No I haven't finished yet,
This evening at five forty,
I am going to the *vet!*

I will have my boost injection,
So that I won't get ill,
And also, (just you hear this),
I must have a worming pill!

I haven't got a little worm,
I woof and huff and shout,
Sshh, says Mum, we must protect
The children hereabout.

The Vet, he is a kind man,
Mum will ask him, with a frown,
'Please will he trim her claws,
Walking hasn't worn them down.'

Am I glowing, healthy, fit?
Can we all play without fear?
A happy little bouncing dog -
Till March again, next year.

I J Wickert

ODE TO AN OLD CAT

We have had you for so long
That we've forgotten
Just how old you now must be.
Fifteen, sixteen, all of that
Our beautiful beautiful tabby cat.

A faithful friend you've always been
And true, no lust to wander.
You speak to us in your own way
Although you seem to sleep all day

Your dainty paws twitch while you
Dream the days away
In chasing shadows.
Your bones are stiff, your muscles weak
It takes you all your time
To climb up on my knee,
But you manage it

And your lovely sleek fur shines
As soft as it has always been
Your tiger markings are as fine
Despite your age.

I hope that when your day is done
We find you in your bed,
Sleeping the long sleep
Of the dead
So that I never have to say
Put her to sleep.

June Thompson

YOU THINK YOU'RE SO SUPERIOR

you think you're so superior
looking down on me
yet I get two meals a day
and both of them are free
I don't start wars
I'd never kneel for you
you think you're so superior
but you haven't got a clue

you think you're so superior
with all your technology
I don't need a mobile phone
to communicate with me
I don't complain about money
and the welfare state
you think you're so superior
but you don't lick your plate

you think you're so superior
patting me on the head
giving me a scratching pole
making sure that I'm well fed
you tell me that you love me
just nine lives and a name
you think you're so superior
but you - you're all the same.

B P S Weldon

TOBY

I like to scratch the paper
And get up to lots of other caper

I knock the odd ornament over here and there
Well why should I care

I am the master of the house
And one day I'll catch that cheeky mouse

Now, I like to think I've got pedigree
Well there's nobody quite like me

I suppose now myself I should introduce
I am Toby, the purrfect wonder puss.

Anne R Cooper

IN SALLY'S EYES

In Sally's eyes if you look deep
Those brown eyes tell a tale
How kindness changed her destiny
When as a pup a fall of fate
Decided racing could not be
For this young, special greyhound
In Sally's eyes a special man could see
How he could turn her life round
So with his care she walked again
Then, yes in time she ran
Though not on tracks but fields back then
Staying loyal to this special man
Two years passed then one sad day
Sally could not understand
Why God had to take her master away
How she pined for that special man
Eleven years old now but in Sally's eyes
Still a sad look always there
Hard living without him in our lives
Though his family know in spirit he's there
Those fields of gold he'd let her run
We still will take her there
In Sally's eyes she sees the love
She knows how much we care
Although no races she has won
In Sally's eyes she's won much more
Her master's home is still the one
Where she will always stay for sure.

Tracy Brierley

MY BORDER COLLIE

I sat on the floor
And crying put my arms around you,
Tears tumbled into your glossy fur,
You alone understood my anguish.
We knew there was no answer to my grief,
I just needed your closeness,
And as your sad eyes gazed into mine,
I found peace,
Then acceptance; gradually filling my soul
Leaving less room for the heartbreak
That had engulfed me.
At last I could begin to live again;
For I knew in your own way
You had been there too and survived.

Christine Clark

PIG

The lunch time beer
Sloshes around the mind
Keeps thinking at bay until at least
Tea time.

The end of the gun barrel
Stretches from the eye,
Wobbling like a fairground ride,
On and off

Of the pig's head.
The creature squeals, helpless,
At the end of its undemanding
Life's script.

Why would it put
Up a fight to live in this
Word where higher intelligence
Equals greater cruelty?

Pig, you made a difference
To me.

Mike Parker

I Follow A Dog's Behind

They look with wicked eyes
At me who they adore
Caring not for my weary sighs
As with leads I make toward the door
In leaps and bounds they race
I follow at a snail's pace
They love the wind if it blows and roars
I follow and the rain it pours
In snow they run and play with ease
Me I follow and freeze
There they go running on ahead
God I wish I was tucked up in bed
One dog is not enough
I have two and I'm out of puff
For all the aches and pain
You will find me here, tomorrow again
For I follow a dog behind.

E C Inkpen

Pussy Cat

Pussy cat, pussy cat
Where have you been?
I know you've been to London
I know you've seen the Queen.
Did she treat you kindly?
Did she give you milk?
No doubt you turned your nose up
But then you felt the guilt
When home you turn -
and wander back
Just think what you will find
Your mistress waiting for you
With a very worried mind.

J Mary Kirkland

MY FRIEND SIMON

I know you're small
and some don't care,
but you're my friend
I'm always there,
your little eyes
they shine so bright
you sleep by day
and play by night
to me you're such
a special friend
I'll love you till
the very end
You listen when I
want a chat
Even though you're
just a *rat.*

Babs West

EPITAPH FOR ROLI

Goodbye Boy Boy
Gone to rest
We'll miss you Roli
Of Britain's best.

No bouncing doggie
Yet in quietness
Your loyalty
Came through.

Patricia Weitz

THE DACHSIE PACK

In days gone by we were only three,
but we called ourselves 'the pack'.
That was before our peace was shattered
by the coming of young Crackajack.

We girls are fourteen, eight and seven,
so an eight week pup upset our life.
What's more he thinks he is clever too,
but we know he causes plenty of strife.

A telephone directory, and thesaurus he chewed,
we thought he was a real little thug,
However, our Jack's now dangerous
with his liking for electric plugs.

When Mum goes out everything's switched off,
and in the kitchen we all have to stay.
Whereas before, we three dear ladies
on the settee were allowed to lay.

Our names are Violet, Amie and Minkie,
and you know he is Crackajack,
We're all cheeky wire-haired dachshunds
who love being part of a pack.

This new member twists us all round his paw,
and we know he has come to stay,
For he is now five months old, and very bold,
so we're teaching him all our own bad ways.

We've worked it all out - we look innocent -
let his lordship take all the blame.
We just have to put up with the scamp -
'Jack the Ripper' is his present name.

Betty Robertson

TSARA

Excitedly wagging pawing the floor I wait my fated call -
Who will choose me make me the Belle of the Ball?
Who'll run after me twenty four hours a day -
Who'll teach me how to really play?
Who'll faithfully follow wherever I go -
Who'll teach me who's friend who's foe?
Who'll fetch me fresh meat and chicken every day -
Who'll know when I have to *stay?*
Who'll be quiet and kind when I go to bed -
Who'll never say he's got a bad head?
Who'll worship the ground on which I walk -
And answer the phone when I can't talk?
Who'll forgive me when I've done wrong -
And promise not to sing me his favourite song?
Who'll let me run o'er hill and dale
And not mind when I've chewed his favourite mail?
Who'll play my games of nip and bite
Get down to my level - have a fight?
Who'll have the wit and wisdom to sense my needs -
And let me share whenever he feeds -
A sliver of liver or two will do
Keep me alert keep me true
The most precious thing to me
Is to let me sit on your knee
And not be upset when I suddenly wet
Calling for help from the nearest vet!
In return I'll try to be good - if only I could . . .
Your forever faithful friend and protector -
I love the snazzy name - Lots of slobbery kisses
Tsara.

Paula Fox

NEW THING

A new addition to our house,
Two ears, four feet and a tail!
Four cats sit and stare at this 'thing'
then they grumble and wail.

A glare, a spit, a growl and a moan,
each cat in a different direction,
then slowly they reappear again.
This 'thing' is far from perfection.

A tennis ball head and little bat ears,
a coat all tattered and torn,
big googly eyes and short little tail.
this 'thing' looks oh so forlorn.

But friendly it is, beyond belief,
our cats are all very wary
of this new, odd shaped 'thing' in life.
Number six cat called 'Miss Mary'.

Susan Ann Higgs

TO BETH

Dear Beth, you came to me a frightened thing,
Beaten and cruelly treated, with neglect:
O bless the unknown man who rescued you,
And cared for you until you came to me.

At two years old, you'd had no puppyhood:
It was a year before you learned to play
And gathered confidence: and that was when
We knew that you loved music, for one night

The close-up of an opera singer showed
Upon the television screen: you licked her face!
I only had to play and sing, and you
Went bounding round the room so happily.

And you loved Master, and would go and sit
And place your golden head upon his knee:
I sat upon the stair-top, and you came -
Your head upon my shoulder, lovingly.

So ten years passed in glad companionship
'til you were ill, and, sadly, girl, you died
My tears fell fast: 'Only a dog' they said:
Ah no! Not only a 'dog' - you were our friend.

Mary Ford

OUR DOG BESS

She was a rescue dog, from the age of four,
Her coat was thin, her behaviour poor,
But with patience and with loving care
Her behaviour grew good, so did her hair -

She is a long legged female, her eyes are big and bright,
She loves romping in the woods, -
Likes a warm bed at night.

She expects her food served on time,
She really is no slouch,
Sometimes if we're not looking she will creep onto the couch.

She really is a beauty, in her coat of black and white,
She never disturbs us when we are sleeping in the night.
We cannot resist her when she for our attention press,
She is now a member of our family, is our dog Bess . . .

Daisy Ellen Jones

MY CAT

My cat, that sits on the mat
Looking so good and so sleek
Really is a little imp
Here's what he did last week
Dug up plants in the garden
Knocked my best vase from the shelf
Brought home a dead mouse for me
Proud he had caught it himself
Jumps out at me as I pass
Tights last me no time at all
Follows me upstairs and down
He drives me right up the wall
But he's mine and I love him
And I hope he loves me too
I will feed him of the best
Yes that is what I'll do.

Dora Watkins

FLOSSY

A dog named Flossy was part of our memorable childhood.
Abandoned early one morning on a lonely rock,
By the beach, curled up asleep in our neighbourhood,
So sad to see her left alone, cold and hungry, shivering in shock.

She looked like a little bundle of fluff,
All black and cuddly and very quiet and rough,
We picked her up and carried her off to our home
And she became our pride and joy, never far from home did she roam.

She looked sad and lonely when we ran off to school
And was always there to welcome us back home was her rule,
No matter where we went she followed us around
And she always felt at home on our solid ground.

Flossy was our pet, a companion and faithful to the end,
When we were young thru her we knew the true meaning of a friend,
But one day we knew the end was near,
Our life was so complete because of her, so to lose her was our fear.

Then that day arrived, those big brown eyes fell asleep,
Gathering around her, we said a prayer and had a little weep.
Then we carried her to our garden where we laid her down to rest,
We laid a plaque that said 'Here lies the one and only and the best'.

Beryl Sylvia Rusmanis

FOR MISHKA AND SASHA (MY BEAUTIFUL CATS)

If I should ever have to leave
And not return to you
It was nothing you have done
Or anything you do.

However much we love another
It's known from the start
One or other in that love
May break the other's heart.

I would ask you - don't be sad
Or, not for very long.
It would be the part you see
Not my love that's gone.

Someone would come to save you
Look after you with care.
Sometimes remember if you would.
But be happy, my dearest dears.

Anita Richards

MY DOG DUKE

My dog Duke
Is not a wild animal
If you love them
They give you so much love back

I got him as a pup
At six weeks old
And now he is six years old
But o' what a dog I love him
He is everything he's my best friend
He listens when I talk
He is with me when I'm lonely
He cheers my every day

I know all his ways
When he's not well
I take him to the vet's
I play with him
O' by the way he is a German Shepherd dog

He is a big dog
But he's so gentle as a lamb
We are the best of pals
To my loving dog how I love you.

M W Lowe

MY SPECIAL FRIEND

I remember that day when you first came into my life,
Bouncing around and checking every corner.
You ran around so hard and so fast,
You panted as if in a sauna

You helped me through my toddler years,
And my nerve-racking, first day at school.
And whenever we would go outside,
We'd always play the fool.

Then the day of bad news came,
When my sister and I were told.
You had cancer and you were dying,
Partly because you were old.

And now in my teenage years,
You're not here in my life with me,
And every day my heart grieves for you,
As I'm sure you can see.

Emma Gale

Gazehounds

I like to watch the elegance and grace
The movement and conformation of dogs that race
Symmetry beholding to the eye
The sheer elegance could make you cry
Whippet and greyhound as they parade around
Like spectre ghosts without a sound
Nothing there could kinder be
To stand with its chin upon your knee
Makes you wonder in the human race
That only a dog should have such an honest face.

Francis Arthur Rawlinson

DEVA

There's a cat upon my bed,
she's lounging there instead,
of dozing on the boiler
in the warm utility.

She's a Burmese bum, my cat,
but I love her, for all that,
she's my solace
in the aftermath of grief:

my beloved died, you see,
and my cat gives sympathy,
she soaks up sorrow
like a handkerchief.

So, we're friends
for all our days,
no matter where she lays,
on my bed, or underneath
a garden tree:

- tail-chasing squirrels
- she never catches -
with a surge of energy,
or just -

stretched out on that boiler,
her most favoured sanctuary.

June Burden-White

MY LITTLE CATS

My heart is as a feather,
Drifting through the air.
No clouds on my horizon,
Do I see anywhere.
My feet don't touch the ground,
As I tread on life's highway.
For into my life has come,
Love that is here to stay.

Those amber eyes that looked at me,
With feelings of distrust.
Now seek me out each morning,
Their welfare to entrust.
Their coats are soft as velvet,
Though silken to the touch.
They've put their trust in me,
And in return they don't want much.

Food to nourish their bodies,
A place to lay their heads.
Shelter from the cold wet nights,
A hand to stroke their heads.
I feel the warmth from their bodies,
Lulling me to sleep.
And when I rise each day,
Know they're mine to keep.

M Muirhead

LUCKY

He lay so still, there was no sound
A ball of fur on the ground
Bleeding and sore, no pads on his feet
He'd walked for miles in the summer heat
No food or friends for at least ten days
Taken for a fox, in the sun's haze.
His coat was terribly matted
Hadn't seen a brush or comb
Surely someone missed him
When he never returned home.
But he had been abandoned, well
That's what we were told
Fancy being turned out of your home
And only six years old.
We nursed him back to health again
He never made a fuss
We knew in our hearts, he would have
Died if it hadn't been for us.
Such a lovely Collie, faithful through
And through. We're very proud to own
Him, we think you would be too.
We've called our dog 'Lucky'
An appropriate name you see
One day perhaps you'll meet him
Then we think you would agree.

S A Buckingham

FIDELIS

He's my little buddy, my best friend,
always there for me.
Always waiting as I'm waking up,
In sleep he's company.
Others says he's just a cat,
my heart knows that's not true.
Him and me both know so much
after all we've both been thru.
In the days when I was very sad
and tears coursed down my face.
He became my counsel, comforter
till my tears he had erased.
'Twas then I thought he was no cat,
think he forgot it too.
Once he had dried my tears for me
he showed me what to do.
There are moments when he makes me mad,
when he wants his way.
Have learned that I must wait for him
'cos he won't do what I say.
He measures up to One foot tall,
but he grows from time to time.
That's when he makes my mountains move
and I am glad he's mine . . .

Rosie Hues

DADDY AND THE FISH

I sit so patiently and wait
For that creak of garden gate
Drivers slam a hundred doors
But I know which one is yours
Through the darkness I can see
So you have no escape from me
I know your footsteps and your smell
Each routine known all too well
I've had a very busy day
Hiding all my toys away
Chasing leaves around the trees
Pawing spiders, bugs and bees
I caught a present just for you
Which I've hidden in a shoe
The sparrow put up quite a fight
By now he should be dead alright
So as my chores have all been done
My little body spent of fun
I sit beside my empty dish
To wait for Daddy and the fish.

Terry Cutting

BEAUTY

What a lot of joy you get
When you decide to have a pet
Particularly when you live alone
And spend hours on your own.

I have a lovely budgie boy
Who has brought me a lot of joy
His antics amuse me very much
Although he talks double Dutch.

His colours are black, yellow and green
I try my best to keep him clean.
Each day he has clean water and seed.
You soon find he's easy to feed.

He is good company all the day
Although he hasn't much to say
When I feel sad he cheers me on
From morn till night when day is done.

He likes singing and dancing on TV
And rings his bell with greatest glee
So if you want a little pet
A budgie is the one to get.

Evelyn M Rose

SNOWBALL CAME

A new baby was expected
What joy! Not for the boy,
'I'd rather have a puppy' he said
This could not be.
A compromise was made.

The birth day came
A wee babe was born
As a white rabbit lay out in the shed
Joy for the boy.
'I name her Snowball' he said.

As he groomed her soft white wool
He told her his troubles and joys,
'You are my best friend, Snowball' he said
Now the baby is here
Together we will share

You'll see.

Dolly Harmer

THE ADORABLE SIX

My cats are the adorable six
And I love them all
To choose a favourite!
Would be - impossible.

Sandy - is a red tabby cat
Who cries if left alone for long
Always sitting on my lap
He loves a lot of attention.

The black and white one is called Cutie
Bigger than all the others, but not fat
Wags her tail thinking she is a doggy
Don't know I got her, she is a sleepy cat.

With a coat so black she is a beauty,
Under her chin is a blob of white
She loves any foods that are milky
Lucy - so graceful, placid and quiet.

Penny - the silver and grey tabby
Is so full of energy, always racing around
Chases balls of paper to bring back to me,
Loves hiding so she can't be found.

The British blue pedigree - his name is Bobby
He looks so intelligent with his big orange eyes,
Mixes with the others now, but once was too snooty,
Talks a lot and makes noises that sound like sighs.

Tammy - is the tortoiseshell with a coat of many colours,
She is so tiny, sometimes I call her titch,
When stroking her she makes such loud purrs,
Always on the move, won't sit still such a fidget.

So much happiness my cats give me
And lots of love and licks
Without them I'd be lonely
My loveable, adorable, six.

Linda Roberts

THIS DOG

This dog's in my bed once again.
It really is getting a pain.
It's led on my toes,
I know that it knows,
To keep out - my training's in vain.

It has its own bed on the floor.
But it just wants that little bit more.
To crawl under the down.
It creeps round and round.
I think I will show it the door.

In the cold light of dawn,
From its bed it has flown,
Straight into my bed,
In spite of what's said.
It comes with a moan and a groan.

What will I do with this dog,
Who sleeps on my feet like a log.
It's really persistent,
And most insistent,
And will this bed of mine hog.

This dog would not give an alarm
She's supposed to keep me from harm.
She's supposed me to guard.
But she's just trying hard,
To keep herself cosy and warm.

Jean Turner

BOB

Sue didn't skate into Bob's world,
he gatecrashed into hers
And she resented his intention.

She treasured her own leisurely
life, besides, his great height
And wide clothes were an embarrassment.

He wore a baggy charcoal coat
over a loose white vest
And his best socks resembled Tesco's.

Long legs crossed, he stretched in awkward
repose, with sketchy thoughts
That kept him lost for words.

One foot, as a rule, pointed west
when he moved, and he stood
Like a piece of Poole pottery.

Bob was an odd fellow in love,
who asked nothing of Sue
And his patience slowly brought reward.

She began to depend on his
Friendship and support.
His adored wardrobe remained the same.

Today, they make a great couple.
Bob is Sue's champion,
Partner and mate: top dog in her world.

Hild

It's A Dog's Life

I take the lead - I am a star
My master shows me near and far.
He barks at me and makes me mad
When I bark back, I'm awfully bad.

I do my best but he chews the rag
He wants the trophy . . . in the bag,
Around the ring I strut and stroll
My head held high, I'm on a roll.

I wag my tail . . . my master smiles
With cup in hand we walk the aisles,
I've done the shows, it must be said
'Drink from the cup, I'm Champion Jed!'

Robert Jennings-McCormick

'TIT-BITS' (BY 'BOUNTY' GUIDE DOG PUPPY AGED 6 MONTHS)

I am sitting and waiting expectant
as you eat your chocolate ice-cream
couldn't you spare me a little bit?
Then you won't seem so mean.

If I sit here looking cute
with my head tilted on one side
perhaps you could make an exception
and give me a bit off the side!

It looks very cool and tempting
and it's disappearing fast,
I'd really like to try it
I don't mind eating the last . . .
little bit!

I don't believe it has gone now
Oh well, I can't win 'em all
I'll have to make do and lick fingers
then dash off and play with my ball.

Lynda Burton

JESSIE 'FAITHFUL FRIEND'

How can I begin to explain your beauty, presence and grace?
The glorious joy you bring to us, with every expression on your face
Each and every day you have been here, you've filled our lives
with Love
Such wonderful feelings we share with you, were you sent to us
from above?
I remember the day we brought you home, a baby - just five weeks old!
You never destroyed anything . . . Just like now, as 'good as gold'
You never speak, yet we understand, all that you want to say
You know that there's a time and place for you to have your play!
If we think of the past before you, it's impossible to realise
How we lived a day without you, when we look into
those big, brown eyes
Imagine in the distant future, unbearable grief we must endure
On the day you have to leave us, will be the hardest for us to bear
But just as in this life we've shared, we have given you our best
On that dreadful day, we will know, our 'faithful friend'
has peace and rest
We will never let you suffer, you deserve the best . . . and more
Dear Jessie, Heaven will be very blessed, when you knock on its door!
But many years we hope to have yet, you delightful, beautiful soul
Continuing to Love and enjoy each day, will be our only goal
Jessie, the very name brings a smile, of that you know it is true
We *never* expected to have a *dog* - as wonderful as *you!*

Christine Peers

EULOGY FOR A FELINE PERSON

I know a worthy feline person
Who's dignified and wise;
He's taught the world to do his bidding -
Success is no surprise.

Yet he's a warm and purry person:
He'll deign to give his love
To all the staff in his employment,
Whose service he'll approve.

So, privileged to have his friendship,
I strive at every turn
To see His Lordship's truly happy
And all his needs discern.

Society of furry persons
Gives mundane life a lift -
The sight of all their many virtues
A tonic that is swift.

The character of feline people
Is noble, kind and shrewd:
Perceptive in all situations,
They'll understand your mood.

I'd recommend a feline person
To listen to your ills,
For there is no one so proficient
In therapeutic skills.

Anne Sanderson

HIT AND RUN

The cat's corpse stretched in one long line,
Laid on the bright grass. He was a fine
Friend, from a trembling scrap of fluff
To this day, which saw a fast car snuff
Life from the lithe-limbed body, full of grace,
So perfect still, but for the tender face,
Where in the rosebud pink a ruby red
Was stopped in death before it even spread.

Brave creature, you will never leap again
To catch butterflies or box the drops of rain,
Nor start like a coiled spring after unseen prey,
Or paddle fastidious paws on a sultry day.
One chance only do you have, small soul,
Before into blank eternity you roll.
Grief grips hard for the brief life shed
Too soon, raw as that stain of ruby red.

Andria Cooke

ALMOST A LION

Orange and proud,
prowling and purring,
arrogant, aloof, mystical -
alluring.
Lets me live with him,
I deem it an honour.
Creature of the night,
green eyes reflecting,
dashing and darting,
sometimes rejecting.
Soft fur and affection,
rubbing and caressing.
Warm fireside companion,
paws twitching.
A welcoming presence
on cold winter evenings,
alarm clock friend
and comic.
All knowing and naughty,
playful and haughty.
Almost a lion.

Audrey Woodall

GOOD DOG, NICE DOG!

'When Adam lived and time began
God sent his canine gift to man.
I came to him: his first best friend
To love and serve him . . . to the end.'

'So Lord, I keep my watch with faith
For you and I know what faith is.
If I'm not here who'll keep him safe
I'll guard his sheep and house that's his.'

'To bring them joy from Lord above
With honest loyalty and love.
To run and play with all my might
I please him, it's my sole delight.'

'When suffering in sad despair,
I'll let him know that I am there.
And come to him and lick his hand
To show him that I understand.'

Gordon P Charkin

Suzi

I was told of a little dog who needed a home,
I went to see her, when I saw this dear little pet
with big brown sad eyes that seemed to say 'Please take me.'
As we met, her fur so thin almost not there,
didn't know what it was to walk on a lead
and meet people, to know household noises
and to feel the softness of grass under her feet.
This I found hard to believe, she was only three,
with all the TLC and patience,
her life is no longer sad but happy.
Suzi who has never looked back
and gives as much love to me and is great company,
my sweet natured Mexican friend
the little long haired Chihuahua.

Gloria A Pocock

INFORMATION

We hope you have enjoyed reading this book - and that you will continue to enjoy it in the coming years.

If you like reading and writing poetry drop us a line, or give us a call, and we'll send you a free information pack.

Write to :-
**Triumph House Information House
Coltsfoot Drive
Woodston
Peterborough
PE2 9JX
(01733) 898102**